GEORGIA'S BRIGHTEST FUTURE INCLUDES RUSSIA

Introduction

The political and economic transformation in Georgia over the past twenty years is nothing short of phenomenal, and should provide hope to any struggling nation that is attempting to modernize. Few could have predicted that a former Soviet state could distance itself from its socialist culture in less than a generation.[1] Though progress continues, for Georgia to achieve its long-term vision of full Western integration, it must first reestablish a normalized relationship with Russia. This renewal of diplomatic relations must begin now, and with an optimistic outlook, it could ultimately resolve the Abkhazia and Ossetia occupation. Georgia has momentum and will continue its path to prosperity, but progress will be more productive if Russia is not motivated to interfere or hinder progress.

Recent political instability in Russia[2] and its upcoming presidential elections in March 2012 represent an outstanding opportunity for Georgia to begin the dialog. This situation is not a time for Georgia to take advantage of a distracted Kremlin. It is long past the time for Georgia to eliminate its overt anti-Russian campaign, soften its public Western rhetoric and embark on a new partnership with Russia. It is important to sustain the positive momentum established during the Russian WTO accession negotiations, and to use the agreement as a springboard to increase goodwill with their northern neighbor. It may seem counter-intuitive for Georgia to emphasize political engagement with Russia during a time when Federation leadership is occupied by higher strategic priorities such as regime survival and economic stability. However, what better time to build relationships than to offer an olive branch when your antagonist is challenged with upheaval and insecurity, and faces the loss of allies and influence in the Middle East?[3] Libyan allegiances are now unknown and Syria and Iran are both under intense domestic or international pressure that threatens their regimes. All could be considered former or current Russian allies. The personal animosity cultivated over the past eight years between Putin and Saakashvili may also telegraph to some that any rapprochement effort should be delayed until the results of the 2012 Russian and 2013 Georgian presidential elections are final, but why wait? The pace of world developments has accelerated greatly, and this window of opportunity is narrow. The strategic situation does not measurably differ between the two countries, even if their leaders do change as a result of elections, so delay offers little benefit. Filow Morar wrote about frozen conflicts: "Time does not necessarily positively contribute to conflict resolution and protracted conflicts are constantly germinating new outcomes and realities, which foments new instances for discontent and conflict." [4] Though some may believe that with strategic patience, Georgia may be able to "wait-out" Russia due to its demographic decline,[5] Russia's energy reserves and intellectual capital give it an excellent foundation to reverse this trend.[6] The geographic reality is that Georgia will never enjoy real security without positive engagement with Russia, no matter how much time elapses. The initiative must come from Georgia. Russia has little incentive to engage Georgia or to make the country more stable, especially now that the WTO hurdle appears to be cleared and Georgia has little leverage at its disposal. Most risks (and potential benefits) of engagement with the Kremlin rest predominantly upon the Georgian people and their leadership, but it is an acceptable and necessary risk. Rebuilding relations with Russia should not alienate Western aid providers, and should serve to improve Georgia's standing with its Western partners.

Russia's South Caucasus Policy

Vladimir Putin's foreign policy has been marked by establishment of a sphere of influence along Russia's borders, and this policy is codified in official Federation documents.[7] Political pressure by NATO, the European Union and the United States to counter the strategy have thus far had limited effect. Georgia must move closer to Russia as a hedge. As with any negotiations with Russia, there are potential obstacles, but Georgia should act. It is possible that Putin could rebuff any new Georgian overtures in an effort to further humiliate Saakashvili in the near term, weakening his United National Movement Party, with hopes of inflicting election losses in 2012/2013. However, these circumstances are already the status quo. There are many options available to the Federation to foment instability in Georgia, and in the entire region.[8] It is in Georgia's interests to ensure these additional steps are not taken. Détente with Russia is the default course of action. There could be some undesirable side effects of increased Russian influence with a new partnership, but an improved relationship with Russia should not automatically signal that Georgia is doomed to the stagnation, interference and corruption that normally permeate Russian satellite societies. In fact, none of Russia's CIS companions have recognized the independence of Abkhazia and Ossetia, so Russia does have limits.

For example, Azerbaijan has managed to keep Russian influence contained,[9] while still maintaining an overall positive relationship with Russia and the United States. Kazakhstan has been one of the more stable relationships for the United States in Central Asia.[10] Armenia has historically been one of the higher per capita recipients of US aid.[11] Even Russia was the 5th largest recipient of US aid from 2000-2008.[12] Just as Armenia, Azerbaijan, Kazakhstan and others do, Georgia can also engage Russia without compromising too much of its sovereignty or Western relationships. The United States does not measurably interfere with any of these sample nation authoritarian governments, and continues to consider them allies, even with very limited Western influence. Georgia could mimic the same strategy. Failure of Georgia to rejoin the Russia Federation umbrella and find the balance between Western development and Kremlin engagement will result in endless instability, similar to the enduring Nagorno-Karabakh and Transnistria conflicts. There must be no preconditions to negotiation. It will be a lost opportunity if Georgia insists that Russia must depart the occupied territories before they establish a dialog.

Georgia should acknowledge that its quality of life will be better with a friendly, but steady Russia, than if it exclusively leans West and continues the antagonistic relationship with their neighbor. It seems a daunting task to achieve Western standards with an aggravated Russia fomenting endless regional instability. This ultimately hinders development and suppresses foreign direct investment. Given the current lack of Western focus on the region, and the lack of Western security assurances (other than financing, training and equipping Georgian forces specifically linked to the Afghanistan mission), Georgia should have plenty of incentive to engage the Kremlin. The lack of political leverage by the EU to measurably influence Russia with soft power also signals that Georgia must accept the inevitability of Russian interference if their relationship remains hostile. Georgia can aspire to Western standards, but they will come much more slowly under the stress of a hostile relationship with Russia, preventing more abundant trade in the region.

As distasteful as establishing positive relations with Russia may seem to many Georgians, a powerful, stable Russia is in their best interest. This applies even if it means Georgia's control of their occupied regions in Ossetia and Abkhazia is a distant dream. For practical purposes, they have not had effective control of these regions since the early 1990s.[13] Focusing on de-occupation and prodding Russia drains resources and hinders foreign investment that could be used to improve the lives of the Georgian people in other ways. A weaker Russia may be more likely to be an irrational/aggressive actor,[14] which could again attempt to manifest its influence

4

and restore perceived lost prestige through military means rather than diplomatic, economic or energy supply pressure.[15] Russian weakness could also embolden many other simmering, but currently more subdued disputes in its regions. If Russia weakens and loses more control of the North Caucasus, for example, former North Caucasus "friends" of Georgia could become problematic, with the elimination of Russia as their common enemy.

Potential Areas of Shared Interests and Risks

There are Georgian risks to an engagement, but ultimately the potential benefits outweigh those risks. Russia could rebuff Georgian overtures, then blame Georgia more intensely for internal Russian problems, arguing Georgians are sabotaging Russia out of revenge for the diplomatic riff. Russian media outlets also insinuate Georgia may assist "terrorists" to disrupt the Olympics (but have provided no proof). But Georgia must still make the effort to engage. Georgia should get back on the path to neighborly relations with Russia, with a few suggestions below:

1. Assuage Russian concerns about terrorism and de-emphasize Georgia's North Caucasus engagement strategy

2. Offer to assist with the Sochi Olympics. Currently, it uses the events and their surrounding publicity as platforms to criticize Russia

3. Address Russian concerns about restored prestige and NATO

4. Reduce the anti-Russian antagonistic rhetoric in official documents and public diplomacy

5. Facilitate Russian Energy Sector Security and Economic Modernization/Development

6. Lower the priority of Ossetia and Abkhazia. Do not make their de-occupation a pre-condition for opening diplomatic relations with Russia

It is feasible that Russia does not want Georgia to succeed under any conditions other than complete subservience, with stifling Russian influence. However, that has not been the case for all other satellites, as mentioned earlier. It could be a challenge for Russia if Georgia becomes too prosperous, as Russia may perceive it as signaling its other near-abroad countries that the West DOES offer a better model. Yet, if Russia could be convinced of the mutual benefits, anxiety could be lowered.

Assuage Russian Concerns About Terror: De-Emphase the N Caucasus Engagement Strategy

Since the late summer of 2008, more representatives of the Russian state were killed in the North Caucasus than US servicemen in Iraq. [16] Seventeen Russians were killed and twenty-four were wounded as recently as February 2012 in the region. [17] Despite the Georgian awareness of Russian sensitivities about the region, Georgia has embarked on a North Caucasus engagement strategy viewed with serious reservations by the Federation. Due to renewed fears of terrorist activities emanating from the North Caucasus, the region is one of the main concerns of the Kremlin and everyday citizens of Russia, This Russian anxiety stems from a seemingly endless chain of events originating in the early post-Soviet period. In the 1980s, the only terrorist attacks recorded in the Soviet Union were 6 hijackings, by people seeking asylum outside the country. [18] But extremism, separatism and terrorism surged onto the radar of Russian leaders when the collapse of the Soviet Union reignited several regional and ethnic conflicts in the former Soviet space. This concern about terrorism was codified in the 2009 publication of the Russian National Security Strategy, and practically implemented in other ways such as with the Shanghai Cooperation Organization charter [19] and some of its sub-institutions. [20] The wars in Chechnya were merely one concern of many, and the North Caucasus instability continues to be a focal point of the Russian leadership.

This concern appears warranted, if you consider the Russian experience since the break-up of the USSR. A plane was hijacked in 1991, but it differed from the incidents of the 1980's because it had the political intent of advancing Chechen independence, rather than a desired end-state of political asylum. It was the beginning of a new phase of violence. A quick review of only a limited number of events since this 1991 hijacking include: Buddenovsk in 1995: a hospital was captured with over 1500 hostages (end result 100+ dead and 400+ wounded at the hands of both Russian forces and terrorists). Pervomayskoye in 1996: the Dagestani border village was stormed where hundreds were killed. Moscow in October 2002: a theater with 920 people was assaulted, and at least 130 hostages died (mostly from a noxious gas pumped into the theater by Russian forces, intended to incapacitate the terrorists, but also killing its citizens). Ingushetia in June 2004: several hundred insurgents attacked Russian government and military facilities. At least 62 were killed by insurgents. Moscow in August 2004: two planes that departed from an airport were destroyed in flight by female suicide bombers, killing 178 people. Moscow, later in August 2004: another female suicide bomber set off explosives at a metro station, killing 10 and wounding 51. And arguably the most infamous incident was Beslan in September 2004: a school was captured with 1100 people (770 children) inside. The eventual death toll was 334, of which 186 were children.[21] More recently, over 30 were killed January 24th, 2011, at the Domodedovo airport in Moscow.[22]

Adding to the insecurity, the Russian leadership faced regional political upheaval simultaneously during this terrorist surge from 2002-2005. Russia experienced political unrest on its borders with the Rose Revolution (Georgia 2003), Orange Revolution (Ukraine 2004), and the Tulip Revolution (Kyrgyzstan 2005).

With this in mind, Saakashvili most certainly understands why the Russian Federation views controlling the Caucasus area as such a critical part of its national security strategy. There are countless other incidents, but these capture the essence of the on-going security challenges. Though many Russian deaths were allegedly caused by the unskilled response of domestic security forces, it has nevertheless ingrained fear in the citizens of the country. Georgia should take steps to increase Russia's sense of security in the Caucasus region, not compromise it.

Lt Gen (Ret) James R. Clapper, U.S. Director of National Intelligence, provided testimony to Congress February 2011, indicating that Georgia's North Caucasus engagement strategy was increasing tensions in the region.[23] He was less emphatic in his January 2012 testimony, merely stating that "the Kremlin has been suspicious about Georgian engagement with ethnic groups in Russia's North Caucasus."[24] Some Georgian endeavors, not specifically outlined by Lt Gen (Ret) Clapper, include piping in political television broadcasts, adopting legislation that could foment potential unrest in the North Caucasus, and granting visa-free entry into Georgia for any Russian citizen from the North Caucasus. The Georgian parliament approved a bill in May 2011 that recognized the Russian empire's attempted extermination of the Circassian people as "genocide." In October of 2010, visa requirements were liberalized for North Caucasians, but this liberalization could have been accomplished without antagonistic policies separating citizens of Russia into different categories. In January 2010, a TV channel called "First Caucasian" began broadcasting from Tbilisi.

The visa regime is a sound policy that brings income into the Georgian economy,[25] but helps to stoke Russian concerns that Georgia may be aiding North Caucasus separatist groups, and therefore increases tensions. It would be prudent to issue visa-free travel to ALL Russians, or visa-required travel for ALL Russians, but separating out citizens of Russia's most volatile regions for special treatment only makes the situation more complicated and increases Russia's suspicion of the outreach effort.

Another possible option to assuage Russian security concerns is to establish a bi-lateral security agreement with Russia for intelligence sharing, similar to the system set up between Russia and its Shanghai Cooperation Organization (SCO) peers. Created in 2004, it is called the Regional Anti-Terrorism Structure, and allows SCO nations to exchange information on terrorist suspects.[26] It facilitates detention and transfer of suspects between SCO nations, and has been compared to some C.I.A. programs administered by the United States.[27]

Georgia should only seek defensive weapons useful for internal defense rather than weapons to defend from external threats, reducing tensions with Russia. If they are convinced they must have more substantial defensive arms, they should consider Russian armaments, so long as their acquisition does not measurably interfere with eventual NATO interoperability. NATO's enlargement requirement indicates a nation must work to achieve interoperability, but it is not a requirement before admission.[28] Though new NATO nations may have suspended most new equipment purchases from Russia, many NATO members still have residual Soviet era equipment that still permits NATO interoperability. This would be a goodwill gesture, to reduce the impact of declining Russian military hardware sales due to lost defense contracts, such as with Libya. Though the arms acquired may not potentially measure up technologically to Western equivalents, they should be sufficient to handle internal disruptions. The weapons are also sufficient for missions such as border protection, should conflict between Armenia and Azerbaijan erupt into a significant refugee situation, or should Iran's political stability cause unrest. There is no need to buy the best military equipment if "good enough" accomplishes the task.

As far back as the 1990s during the Chechen wars, Russia has considered Georgia a supporter of North Caucasus unrest. Russia considered Georgia a safe-haven for combatants during these wars.[29] Georgia must take action to reverse their reputation as historical supporters of unrest. Georgia should immediately cease its overt public efforts to engage the North Caucasus at the expense of Russian stability. Though there are many reasons unrelated to Chechnya for the animosity that exists between Russia and Georgia, this remains a significant friction point. Georgia should remove anti-Russian rhetoric from their television programming on their First Caucasian network, intended for North Caucasus audiences as well as domestic, and stick to positive messages about Georgia and its opportunities. Finally, the Georgian Parliament should not put forth *any* additional legislation aimed at humiliating or antagonizing Russia. The country should leave designations of genocide to impartial historians and not domestic politicians.

Assist with the 2014 Sochi Olympics

Georgia has consistently alleged that Russia is pillaging the resources of Abkhazia to provide the raw materials necessary to prepare for the Sochi Olympics in 2014.[30] Additionally, they have made claims that Russia is leaving significant environmental damage in its wake with its deforestation, cement production pollution and construction waste as a result of these efforts. These claims are supported by a Time magazine article in Fall 2011. [31] Georgia has been using the upcoming Olympics as a platform to criticize Russia and generally disseminate poor publicity about its neighbor. However, this may not be an effective strategy. Though admirable to defend Abkhaz conservation, Abkhazia must resolve this issue with the Russians, as the Georgians have no leverage under the current political situation, and external actors should not interfere with internal Russian affairs. Georgia does not have influence in the matter, despite the fact that Abkhazia is still internationally recognized as their territory. Consistently drawing attention to negative aspects of the Games is counter-productive. Georgia would be better served to offer assistance to ensure Olympic success, rather than continue political rhetoric to sabotage them. No one is suggesting, except with the possible exception of Russia, that Georgia would actually be involved with actions beyond rhetoric to ruin the event. Yet, Russian insinuation has been evident and the Kremlin may claim any Olympic security problems were encouraged by Georgian statements and policy.[32]

Support from Georgia for the event could help negate Russian efforts at implicating Georgia in any future unrest. Georgia chose to initiate the military action in August of 2008 to protect its citizens in South Ossetia during the opening days of the Beijing Olympics, certainly something that has not been forgotten internationally. Georgia's actions to discredit the positive spectacle of the Games at *another* Olympic event will most likely be met with disregard or worse, disapproval, by most nations. Georgian efforts to disparage Russia over the Olympics will predictably be without gainful effect, so why attempt to mar the event and risk Georgian public standing in the process. There is nothing to gain but backlash from the International community for politicizing the Olympics, and more animosity with Russia. Additionally, Georgia should take the same positive stance for the 2016 Hockey World Championships and 2018 Soccer World Cup.

Address Russian Concerns about Restored Prestige and NATO

A recent Russian newscast indicated that if the United States or Israel attack Iran, the next domino to fall, counter to their strategic interests, will be Georgia and Azerbaijan joining NATO. Even with a consistent force reduction trajectory in NATO, on-going for decades, and significant U.S. cuts announced to military spending and combat brigades being withdrawn from Europe,[33]

11

Russia continues to perceive and portray NATO as enemy number one. It is debatable whether the Siloviki truly have an ingrained fear of NATO, or whether anti-Western rhetoric simply plays well for domestic politics.[34] If we look at the 2011 Russian parliamentary elections as a possible indicator, it would suggest that the electorate has many concerns of greater importance than NATO, since anti-missile-defense and anti-NATO rhetoric were greatly played up by the United Russia Party. This increased anti-Western rhetoric did not seem to have a significant positive impact on the United Russia Party election results. Nonetheless, whatever the true concerns about NATO, Georgia needs to take steps to assuage Russia's fears about NATO encroachment into the Caucasus region.[35] Despite the potential that Georgia in NATO could actually be beneficial for Russia, resulting in *more* stability on its southern border, the issue is not likely to change, even in the long term.

The real NATO threat to Russia is psychological and symbolic, but it is a situation that Georgia must consider. If NATO expands to the Caucasus, it won't change the likelihood that NATO will attack Russia (current probability at near zero),[36] but Russians may perceive it as "decline" from their Soviet days.[37] They have demanded a "near-abroad" and NATO inclusion of Georgia would be a direct implication that Russia has limited International influence. Georgia must appreciate the position faced by NATO countries, who seek to minimize unrest in the entire world, not just the Caucasus. Georgia should not cease its aspiration to formally join NATO, but it should cease its overt rhetoric. It should engage opportunities to align itself with NATO standards for potential future admission, but more quietly. It is feasible to aspire and take action to achieve NATO standards without formal admission into the organization. Though Russia may be uncomfortable with the U.S. training Georgian forces (demonizing the training and equipping plays well in domestic politics), they must assuredly understand that it is for securing the situation in Afghanistan, which is in their best interest. Russia will continue to tolerate it. Georgia should conduct itself as if non-aligned. It would not be without precedent. Ukraine often conducts military exercises with the United States, yet has retracted its interest in joining NATO and leans more and more toward Russia. Armenia has 80 military-to-military events scheduled for 2012 with the US, and the nation is arguably a Russian satellite. Georgia can operate within those brackets as well.

Georgia should continue to seek EU political and economic expertise for possible integration, but it should also become a less overt foreign policy objective. There appears a smaller risk in EU accession aggravating the Kremlin, as Russia appears more concerned about NATO than the EU. This could possibly be due to the EU's lack of credible military capability and the political will to employ it.

Georgia should make the offer to Russia not to provide material support to any nation that attacks Iran. This is not only in Georgia's interest from a Russian-relations perspective, but from an internal security perspective as well, given their proximity to Iran. They should do this to ensure they don't become an Iranian or Iranian sympathizer's target. The West would accept this reality and not fault the nation. This commitment would not hinder US interests or Western ability to conduct operations in the region, and may give Georgia political top-cover in the case of conflict. Since Georgia has no significant air defense, nations could use their airspace in emergency situations with no risk of air defense encounters.

Georgia should commit that no *permanent* NATO forces will be permitted on Georgian soil, except for training and exercise purposes. This would also be of no detriment to Western interests, since it is highly unlikely that NATO will admit Georgia in the foreseeable future, or that the West has an interest in establishing basing. Why build bases in Georgia when you are closing them in Europe?

Georgia should postpone, without announcement, its NATO accession strategy. Even with strong US support for Georgian admission to NATO, it is a goal located far on the horizon. The US staunchly supports Turkish admission to the EU, but there are too many competing interests in the EU to translate that U.S. pressure into action. US support for Georgia alone, will not overcome NATO objections either.

Though Russia and Turkey have significantly improved relations over the past decade,[38] Georgia should give *private* assurances to Russia that if its interests conflict with Turkey, Iran or others, Russia can count on their support. Turkey offered limited to no support to Georgia politically during the Georgian-Russian conflict in 2008,[39] and Georgia owes them no favors. Turkey did provide financial support after the conflict, and they do enjoy significant amounts of trade with Georgia, but this is an economic marriage and does not come with political or military guarantees. Though Turkey is a NATO member, it would not be the first time Western or Western-leaning nations have not supported Turkey in its foreign policy. Currently there are large disparities in the positions of several nations with respect to Turkey's Cyprus and Israeli policies, for example. Likewise, there has been no progress on Turkey's admission to the EU.

While there has been limited dialog to suggest that the Arab Spring could migrate to the North Caucasus, Georgia should reaffirm to Russia that it will not provide safe haven in the event of further North Caucasus unrest.

Georgia should consider rejoining the Collective Security Treaty Organization as they wait for NATO's embrace. Though it may be unpalatable to the Georgians to do so, they currently have no other alliances that assure them military protection against significant potential external threats, for example if Iran's political condition deteriorates or if an assault on Iran's nuclear facilities causes regional unrest. If Georgia were to become a signatory to this document, it would reassure Russia that Georgia would not allow U.S. or NATO basing on its territory without member-nation clearance. The CSTO charter was recently adjusted to deny basing access in CSTO countries without unanimous CSTO approval.[40] Since the U.S. and NATO have no intention of putting any bases in Georgia, there seems little to lose for Georgia by taking this initiative. This would also assuage Russian concerns that NATO could eventually place missile defense positions on Georgian soil. This does not place Georgia at odds with NATO, since it only covers permanent basing. There are several U.S. or NATO bases in the Central Asian region, in CSTO nations, and none are considered *permanent* at this writing. Georgia's possible alignment with the CSTO is not necessarily at the expense of NATO.

Georgia should not push the NATO accession agenda at the upcoming NATO Chicago Summit in May 2012, and they should absolutely minimize antagonistic references to Russia during the event. There will be other summits. Inflammatory remarks will only give the United Russia Party political fodder for domestic purposes. If Russia is made a focal point at the summit in a negative manner, Russia will continue to dig into their position that NATO is a threat.

Georgia should drop its efforts to obtain Western air defense systems and other equipment that would be a threat to Russia. It would only antagonize Russia. Additionally, Russia can capture the remaining Georgian territory through military action, whether Georgia possesses advanced defensive weapons or not. Tbilisi is too close to current Russian force positions in South Ossetia for the international community to be able to react militarily, even if it had the resolve. If Russia decides that capturing Tbilisi or the remainder of Georgia is in their best interests, they may be slowed but not stopped, even with the Russian military's glaring deficiencies.[41] The de-facto U.S. arms embargo against Georgia[42] has kept the situation from inflaming again, approaching the 4th complete year. No one should seek to destabilize the region by shipping more external arms there.

Reduce Anti-Russian Antagonistic Rhetoric in Official Documents and Public Diplomacy

The Draft National Security Concept of Georgia, recently passed by Parliament, and waiting for Presidential signature, mentions Russia at least 30+ times in the first 8 pages alone (a 28-page document).[43] These references are typically not flattering. Georgia must drastically reduce the rhetoric, as it has resulted in no concrete gains from the international community. It seems that you cannot read an article referencing a Saakashvili speech without hearing about Russia. He seems the master of inserting the Kremlin into any discussion. Nations hear the words, but won't likely change their policies simply because of Georgia's consistent reminders of Russia's aggression in 2008. Eventually, it becomes background noise with gradually diminishing impact. Georgia should shift even more to "back-door" diplomacy, where they raise their points in private meetings rather than in public forums. Continued Georgian rhetoric gives Putin more domestic ammunition that the threat is constant and real from the Caucasus, NATO, and Georgia. The rhetoric can be used to reinforce Russian claims that Georgia's strategy and long-term goal is to destabilize Russia.

Facilitate Russian Energy Sector Security and Economic Modernization/Development

Russian leaders know they need to modernize and diversify their economy,[44] with a keen eye on current and future demographic challenges facing the nation. Conventional wisdom would indicate that fomenting instability in energy markets, therefore supporting higher energy prices, is the best mechanism to ensure sufficient revenues for Russia to effect this modernization.

However, Russia understands that political and economic instability (in Russia and the world) causes capital flight and loss of foreign investors.[45] Georgia, with strong Western support, should continue to reinforce to Russia that peace is in both their economic interests. [46]

Foreign investment and technology are needed for Russia to overcome its economic challenges. But no one will place resources there if the risk is perceived as too high.[47] Georgia can't do anything to help the International community have more faith in Russian observance of the rule of law, but they can help contribute to a better perception of stability in Russia, starting with the South Caucasus.[48] As mentioned earlier, Russia has no significant geo-strategic incentive to normalize relations with Georgia. They have soldiers immediately south of the Caucasus mountain range, and likely want to keep them there. However, if détente between Georgia and Russia will increase investor confidence and direct foreign investment increases as a result, there may be a sliver of hope for normalization. Resolution of the WTO impasse is already a step in that correct direction. Political stability would also improve as the foreign investment starts to materialize and both economies become stronger. Citizens want to see improvement in their lives and security on their borders, no matter where they live or what political system they aspire to join.

Georgia does not appear to offer much in the realm of geographic importance to Russia as an energy transit route to European markets. But if peace with Georgia makes Russia a more reliable energy source than the Middle East, it could slow the EU's pressure for supply diversification, transition to LNG, and unbundling of energy supply vs energy transport companies,[49] all of which can cut into Russian energy profits or potentially reduce Russia's EU energy market share.[50]

No observers predicted that only three years after the war of 2008, Georgia would agree to Russian admission into the WTO. Yet, relatively soon after the war, there exists an agreement.[51] Georgian détente with Russia would make it more likely the Kremlin will adhere to the terms of the WTO Swiss-brokered agreement. Once Russia is admitted to the WTO, there are a limited number of procedures to remove them, even if Russia violates the Georgian agreement. Georgia gains nothing if Russia chooses to ignore the agreement.[52] There could be plenty of opportunities for Russia to subvert the agreements, if relations between the two nations remain strained.

Georgia should re-open the railway linking Russia and Armenia via Abkhazia. Not only for potentially receiving a customs income, but because it would reduce the isolation of Armenia and further stabilize the region and encourage more economic development. Turkey would most likely not consider this a threat or concern. Turkey recently initiated diplomatic efforts to normalize relations with Armenia over the past several years, and most observers recognize the initiative was a failure only because of Azerbaijan's strong opposition, not Turkey's lack of resolve. It is also likely that Turkey would view any initiatives that maintain political stability, and simultaneously increase economic opportunity for Turkey as a positive development. Georgia may risk some Azeri pushback, but could seek ways to tie this rail opening into the greater WTO issue, and this could also actually stabilize the region.[53]

Georgia should formally leave GUAM, the Organization for Democracy and Economic Development (Georgia/Ukraine/Azerbaijan/Moldova). This organization has become essentially irrelevant,[54] and could be perceived as an anti-Russian consortium. Dismantling it would be a sign of goodwill, since its creation was widely recognized as a counter to Russian interests.[55]

Georgia should seriously consider the benefits of joining the new Eurasian customs union with Belarus, Kazakhstan and Russia, until such a time as it would be admitted into the EU. This is currently only an economic block, rather than political or military organization, and should not compromise Georgia's ability to remain non-aligned. This union does not interfere with the WTO charter and would open up Georgian markets immediately to trade with Russia. Even though Georgia has been effective in locating alternate markets for its goods since Russia imposed dubious embargoes on Georgian wine, water and other products starting in 2006,[56] adding the Russian market for goods would increase economic opportunity in Georgia and contribute to an expanding GDP.[57] Joining the customs union could also expand the income associated with Russian tourism. Though Russian tourism is growing in Georgia and represented 8% of their total visitors in 2010,[58] they could benefit greatly if they were able to attract many of the Russians that now extensively go to Turkey,[59] Abkhazia and other destinations.

Georgia may be able to assist Russia to mitigate the natural gas market's paradigm shift to Liquefied Natural Gas, which has seen significant demand increase as nations have announced termination of nuclear energy programs. As competition increases in the gas market, LNG has the potential to interfere with Russia's ability to sell its gas at profitable prices. Georgia could offer the port of Poti or Supsa for development to export Russian gas as LNG.[60] This could help Russia diversify its delivery options away from its principally fixed pipeline method, and better compete with the U.S. and others that are greatly expanding their gas extraction abilities. Georgia could also offer to serve as a transit route for Russian gas to the already existing LNG facility at Ceyhan, Turkey. Georgia may then be able to negotiate lower gas prices from Russia as relations improve, though Georgian dependence on Russian gas has dropped significantly from 2008, to a current 14% of total imports.[61]

More incentive for Georgia to move quickly, to become relevant in the Russian energy sector, is the recent Turkish approval of the South Stream pipeline. It is in the process of development after Turkey granted territorial rights to Russia to run the pipeline through its littoral areas of the Black Sea.[62] There is some professional debate about whether this pipeline will come to fruition, since some see it as an economic ploy to coerce Ukraine into selling its pipeline system to Russia. If this pipeline is actually built, with current estimates placing it operational in 2015, this makes fruition of the Nabucco pipeline less likely, and therefore reduces the opportunity for Georgia to collect increased transit fees that would have ensued, were Nabucco to materialize. With the North Stream pipeline already functional between Germany and Russia, this new pipeline will further cement EU reliance on Russian energy sources and reduce the likelihood that the EU has the ability to put any measurable pressure on Russia over Georgian issues.

The longer Georgia waits to engage Russia, the more leverage that Russia gains over the EU because of energy and trade dependence, which will put Russia in a stronger position to completely rebuff any Georgian overtures. The situation is already tough for Georgia. Three nations out of Europe's four biggest economies have reasonably close ties to Russia. Germany is heavily dependent on the North Stream gas pipeline and billions in trade from Russia. France is selling Mistral amphibious ships to the Kremlin[63] and Italy's former Prime Minister brags that a recent bruise he displayed was caused by a hockey match with Putin.[64] The EU is becoming more and more intertwined economically, and in some cases personally, with Russia and its leaders.

Georgia should offer to assist Russia by sharing its police anti-corruption expertise. Though it is highly unlikely that Russia would accept such assistance in the short term, many CIS nations have been sending delegations to Georgia to obtain lessons learned on their anti-corruption campaign. Russia could eventually acquiesce.[65]

Lower the Priority of Ossetia and Abkhazia

Georgia must contemplate existence without Abkhazia and South Ossetia. If England can forgive America after it declared independence and tossed the British from North America, if Russia and Germany can be on good terms after WWII, if Vietnam and the USA can normalize relations, and if Afghanistan can work with Russia after the debilitating war in the 80s,[66] then Georgia can lift itself above the occupation topic and engage Russia. The situation will not resolve itself without engagement. Though these are clearly not identical situations, no two conflicts are alike, and in fact, the United States did not give any 'occupied' land back to England after the Revolutionary War. England could easily argue that the United States is occupying lands that are historically theirs, but they do not.

Some will argue that on-going territorial occupation resulting in hundreds of thousands of displaced citizens is more egregious than the killing of millions in wars decades ago. However, it is hard to equate any offense higher than the tens of millions killed between Germany and Russia, and Russia's subsequent annexation of parts of Germany for 40+ years after WWII. Those countries are considered friends now by most observers. Georgia can also overcome the unpleasant aspects of their history with Russia as well.

It was possibly a political miscalculation on President Saakashvili's part to make controlling the territories a central tenet of his political platform. However, Medvedev and Putin may have actually done Saakashvili a favor by declaring the regions independent, thereby transferring all of the instability, risk and financial exposure to Russia, away from Georgia. If Georgia were to cede their rights to these regions, it would eliminate the border dispute, and perhaps pave a more expeditious path to eventual acceptance into either NATO or the EU. Ceding these territories does not mean they can never return to Georgia. But, Georgia should be cautious and temper expectations, as solving its border disputes with Russia is only one of many other hurdles remaining to NATO or EU admission. Georgia did everything within its capability to protect the Georgians in these regions and to keep their territory, including facing off with the full military force of Russia. But it is a losing proposition for any nation confronting such a huge numerical hurdle, and that numerical disadvantage will not change. Without security guarantees from other nations, Georgia is at Russia's mercy.

The territories do not currently want to join Georgia, and force won't solve this. Georgia has offered various versions of political autonomy to the regions over the years, but none have resonated with the population. Assimilating the territories may not work, even if their populations do reconsider their alignment. Several European leaders have recently decried multi-culturalism as a failure. If Abkhazians and Ossetians don't consider themselves Georgian, there seems more to lose than gain, by re-annexing them. Ossetia is an economic and social challenge with a small population, rampant crime and few developmental prospects. Abkhazia is a different situation in many respects, but there are no signals that there is current interest on the part of its citizens to rejoin Georgia. Beyond these, there is also no "face-saving" way for Russia to reverse its independence recognition.

Saakashvili is the only former Soviet republic head of state which the Kremlin refuses to engage. Some predict there could be Russian overtures to Georgia upon Saakashvili's departure from his post (assuming he does not move into the Prime Minister's position), but giving back Ossetia and Abkhazia as one of those overtures seems a remote possibility. Having troops permanently south of the main Caucasus range in Georgia's former territories is most likely in their perceived long term strategic interest, since Caucasus regional security is a concern. [67] The likelihood that Georgia could negotiate the return of these regions or even eventually integrate them without first normalizing relations with Russia is very poor. As a potential incentive, Georgia should consider reaching an agreement with Russia to get the territory back under Georgian control, but granting phased basing rights to Russia, allowing their military bases. This may seem like a set-back from 2007, when Russia pulled out its remaining troops from Georgian soil, but Russia's troops are there now. Departure dates can be negotiated later. These basing rights should not necessarily be permanent, and their duration could be renegotiated at established times. Kyrgyzstan hosts both NATO and Russian troops, and Georgia could do the same if the security situation demanded it in the future.

Some may suggest that Georgia can attempt to make their example of government and rule of law attractive to the break-away regions…."a beacon of light that attracts Ossetia and Abkhazia back to Georgia"…..but Russia would likely not allow this under the current hostile diplomatic climate. It would signal all their former satellites that leaving the Russian sphere is the most enlightened option. This "beacon" policy should be considered a very long term goal. Ethnic demographics in these regions are a challenge. If Russia surprisingly turned a blind eye to Georgia's development and chose not to interfere, there is still not much ethnic motivation for the break-away region's citizens to rejoin Georgia, since almost all ethnic Georgians left the two zones in the 90's or more recently in 2008. There isn't a Georgian Diaspora in these regions to pressure local politicians, so there is little attraction. The regions are lost to Georgia for the foreseeable future, and Georgia should be prepared to advance without them. Georgia was not an independent nation for more than a few years over the past two hundred years between 1800 and 1990. Georgia did not have control of Abkhazia and South Ossetia for at least 20 years, so it is a tough challenge to say they were taken by force in 2008, when they were essentially already gone.[68] International recognition does not alter this reality.

Conclusion:

Georgia must reengage Russia without preconditions, especially the de-occupation of Abkhazia and Ossetia, while maintaining close but more subtle contact with the West. It cannot rely solely on Western institutions to ensure its economic development and cannot expect Western assurances of its physical security. They should manage their expectations with respect to Western aspirations and shift towards normalizing diplomatic relations with Russian. Of course, this path has risks, since Soviet attitudes and politics still permeate some of the post-Soviet space, but risks of inaction are greater. Western goals will never be realized with consistent Russian interference as a result of Georgian antagonism. Additionally, the West lacks national interests significant enough to assure Georgian security guarantees. Trenin wrote that Russia wanted to have a sphere of interest, but not a sphere of influence,[69] insinuating that Russia does not require a dominant role in its neighbor's affairs, and recent experience in Central Asia and other areas suggest this is feasible.

Individual EU country bilateral agreements with Russia and their dependency on its energy sources and trade markets are problematic for Georgia. The United States has significant budget constraints, a military drawdown, and renewed efforts to tighten relations with Russia, with the view that all nations will benefit, not just Georgia. It is unlikely that the EU has the resources to further the Georgian cause beyond supportive public statements, humanitarian and economic financial aid, and low-impact defensive military hardware. NATO membership must be recognized as a distant goal. There is simply no threat large enough to motivate NATO members to expand the alliance any further under current affairs. Because of these headwinds, Georgia must engage Russia positively to assure their benevolence, while sustaining Western support. This is their best chance to in peace and harmony in a very volatile region. Once Georgia normalizes with both East and West, it will achieve its true potential.

Endnotes:

[1] Rubin, Eric, "The South Caucasus: 20 Years of Independence," Speech at Carnegie Endowment for International Peace Conference, Nov 28, 2011. Paragraph 9, discusses the remarkable transformation in Georgia.

[2] Trenin, D, "Protests in Russia," Dec 29, 2011, Carnegie Endowment for International Peace, wrote that "Russian authorities see the protests as the most serious challenge to their power since taking office in 2000." "Quite a few are haunted by the specter of an Orange Revolution, Russia-style, ordered and orchestrated by Washington."

[3] Klein, Magarate, "Russia and the Arab Spring," Feb 2012, SWP Comments 3, German Institute for International and Security Affairs. Page 6 ""..concern spread that the 'Arabellion' could destabilize Russia.....by spreading Islamism and terrorism in regions like the N Caucasus or portions of Central Asia..."

[4] Morar, Filon "The Myth of 'Frozen Conflicts'" June 2010, per Concordiam, pg 10-17, George C Marshall Center Publication

[5] Stewart, Susan, "A Weaker Russia. Serious Repercussions for EU-Russia Relations," Sept 2011, SWP Comments, German Institute for International and Security Affairs. Page 2 covers Russian decline in infrastructure, population decline, deteriorating health and education services, wage disparity and control of large geography

[6] Goldstone, Jack A, "Rise of the TIMBIs," Dec 2, 2011, Foreign Policy. Mexico is given as an example of a country that overcame its energy dependency for revenue, stating that from 1980 to 2000, oil dropped from 62% to 7% of exports, yet economic growth from 1995 to 2002 was 5.1% average per year. It could be argued that Russia has more intellectual capital available than Mexico, and could therefore escape its energy dependency and reverse its decline as well.

[7] National Security Strategy of the Russian Federation until 2020

[8] Lake, Eli, "Saakashvili: U.S. Stopped Russia Bombings," Sept 26, 2011, TheDailyBeast.com. One of these options to create instability, from the article "A bomb that exploded at the exterior wall of the U.S. Embassy in Tbilisi......U.S. intelligence assessments...conclude the embassy bombing was directed by a Major in Russian Military Intelligence..."

[9] Yepifantsev, Andrei, "Russia in Transcaucasia: What's Gone Wrong?" 24 Sept 2011, Russia in Global Affairs. Article states "The Russians do not have much leverage or influence over Baku"

[10] Roberts, Sean, R, "Kazakhstan and the United States: Twenty Years of Ambiguous Partnership," Atlantic Council ISSUEBRIEF, 2011. Author states that "the most stable and fruitful bilateral partnership for the U.S. in the region over the past 20 years has been with Kazakhstan……there has been on-going cooperation between the two countries in a variety of areas….."

[11] Nichol, Jim "Armenia, Azerbaijan and Georgia: Political Developments and Implications for U.S. Interests," April 15, 2011. Author states: "Armenia and Georgia have regularly ranked among the top world states in terms of per capita U.S. aid." Additionally the New York Sun ran an article in 2005 that stated about Armenia: "Yet this tiny South Caucasus republic receives more American aid per capita than any other country except Israel - a total of more than $1.6 billion since 1992." Located at http://www.nysun.com/foreign/second-largest-recipients-of-us-aid-armenians/18286/.

[12] Schaefer, Brett D and Kim, Anthony B, "U.S. Foreign Aid Recipients Show Little Support for America When Voting at the United Nations," April 6, 2010, Heritage Foundation 'Backgrounder' No 2395. Chart on Page 5 built from info from several US government agencies, shows Russia 5th in aid between 2000-2008, only behind Iraq, Israel, Afghanistan and Egypt.

[13] Jane's Sentinel Country Risk Assessment, Georgia, Executive Summary, National Overview, states: "…Tbilisi's lack of real control over Gerogia's recognized borders since the early 1990s. ….fighting between 1990-1993 left the regions of Abkhazia and South Ossetia outside central government control…."

[14] Kamp, Karl-Heinz, "NATO's Chicago Summit: A Thorny Agenda," NATO Research Paper No 70, November 2011. Author states"…Russia is likely to become progressively weaker…..and could be tempted to compensate for this by becoming increasingly assertive and pushy on the international scene."

[15] Reuters news release in Moscow Times, "Arms Spending A Crutch for Diplomacy," Oct 14, 2011, Ruslan Pukhov quoted as saying "Soft power doesn't work for us. We need people to be afraid of us, and we seem to be unable to find a proper substitute for military power."

[16] Russian Figures show 230 for only 2009. www.en.rian.ru/russia/20100116/157570882.html

[17] Reuters news release, "Russia Clashes Leave at Least 24 Dead in North Caucasus," Feb 18, 2012, Moscow. The 24 dead includes insurgents. When you subtract out the 7 insurgents referenced in the article, it results in the figure of 17 Russian officials dead.

[18] Soldatov, Andrei and Borogan, Irina, "The New Nobility," 2011. Page 179.

[19] http://www.sectsco.org/EN/show.asp?id=69, Article 1, Goals and Tasks

[20] http://www.sectsco.org/EN/AntiTerrorism.asp

[21] Soldatov, Andrei and Borogan, Irina, "The New Nobility," 2011. Page 135-189 go into great detail on several of the incidents mentioned in the paragraph above.

[22] http://www.reuters.com/article/2011/01/24/us-russia-blast-airport-idUSTRE70N2TQ20110124

[23] http://www.dni.gov/testimonies/20110210_testimony_clapper.pdf, Pg 20

[24] http://www.dni.gov/testimonies/20120131_testimony_ata.pdf, Pg 21

[25] Valieva, Elizaveta, "Making Mischief," 2011, Caucasus Security Insight, International Institute for Strategic Studies. Author is anti-Georgian, yet recognizes "Economically, of course, such an opening of the borders in beneficial to the North Caucasus republics as well as to Georgia and even Armenia."

[26] http://www.ecrats.com/en/, Many details of the organization in several sections of web-site

[27] Soldatov, Andrei and Borogan, Irina, "The New Nobility," 2011. Page 221 states that the organization operates "much like the infamous CIA practice of extraordinary rendition."

[28] http://www.nato.int/cps/en/natolive/official_texts_24733.htm, Text states "While new members will not be required to achieve full interoperability with NATO before joining the Alliance, they will need to meet certain minimum standards essential to a functioning and credible Alliance."

[29] Kelkitli, Fatma A, "Russian Foreign Policy in South Caucasus Under Putin," Perceptions, Winter 2008. Page 71 discusses short history of Georgian support to Chechens including harboring refugees, allowing Chechen media outlets to operate in Georgia and the opening of a Chechen Representation Office in Tbilisi.

[30] Corso, Molly, "Georgia and the Sochi Olympics Games" 5 Dec 2011, Caucasus Analytical Digest No 32. Page 5, Author describes transition of Georgian President's position from initial support of Sochi, to boycott discussions, and an eventual policy of propagating bad PR for the event

[31] Thornburgh, Nathan, "Olympic Dreams" Time Magazine, 28 November 2011, http://www.time.com/time/magazine/article/0,9171,2099428,00.html

[32] Corso, Molly, "Georgia and the Sochi Olympics Games" 5 Dec 2011, Caucasus Analytical Digest No 32, Page 6 Author states ""While there are reports Moscow is taking precautions to protect the Game's venues and future guests, rhetoric from Russian officials indicates that the Kremlin is prepared to blame Tbilisi for any problems that occur during the Olympics."

[33] Barnes, Julian E and Hodge, Nathan, "Military Faces Historic Shift," Jan 6, 2012, Wall Street Journal, discusses Army reductions from 570,000 to 490,000 soldiers and the new US emphasis on Asia vice Europe.

[34] The Economist, "Russia and NATO, an Absence of Trust," Nov 19, 2011, article states "Russian military analysts concede that the phased approach to European missile defense.......even in its final phase....would be overwhelmed by any Russian attack." Besides NATO expansion to Russia's borders, missile defense is probably the most contentious issue, and many Russian analysts concede it is not a real issue.

[35] National Security Strategy of the Russian Federation until 2020, The document does not mention Georgia specifically in this context, but does state: "A determining aspect of relations with NATO remains the fact that plans to extend the alliance's military infrastructure to Russia's borders.....are unacceptable to Russia...."

[36] Rasmussen, Anders F, Speech by NATO Secretary General, 17 December 2009, he stated: "NATO will never attack Russia. Never. And we do not think Russia will attack NATO."

[37] National Security Strategy of the Russian Federation until 2020. There are many references in differing language, intended to evoke the return of Russia's global importance. Only one example being "....the enhancement of the ...international status of the Russian Federation.....

[38] Karasar, Hasan A, "Turkey and Russia Growing Closer Despite Cool History," Jan 30, 2012, The German Marshall Fund of the United States, Author states "...recent warm relations between Ankara and Moscow have ensured a more multi-polar and Eurasian world order. Other references show that about 3 million Russians visit Turkey each year as tourists, and Turkey is heavily reliant on Russian Energy....all steering both nations to closer ties.

[39] Karasar, Hasan A, "Turkey and Russia Growing Closer Despite Cool History," Jan 30, 2012, The German Marshall Fund of the United States. Author states "The 2008 Georgian-Russian conflict was the point when Russians really started to trust Turks since Turkey took a 'neutral' attitude." Several other observers noted that Turkey was careful not to make anti-Kremlin statements during and after the war, not wanting to risk relations.

[40] Racz, Andras, "Good Cop or Bad Cop? Russian Foreign Policy in the New Putin Era," January 2012, Transatlantic Academy, Author states: "The charter of the CSTO was recently modified in such a way so as to prohibit any member state from hoting a foreign military base on its territory without the consent of all other CSTO members."

[41] Reuters news release, "Arms Spending A Crutch for Diplomacy," October 14, 2011, Moscow Times, article states "the call for military reform.....stems from problems in conflicts stretching from failure in Afghanistan in the 1980s to the embarrassments suffered in a five-day war with Georgia in 2008."

[42] Talev M and Bedwell, H, "Obmam Says U.S. May Explore Georgia Trade Pact as Country Seeks NATO Entry," January 30, 2012, Bloomberg News, article states "Obama, in his public comments, didn't make any commitment to sell arms to Georgia as the country has requested." Though there is no official US policy that forbids arms sales, it is widely known that advanced defensive weapons have not been provided to Georgia.

[43] Government of Georgia, "Georgia National Security Concept," Tbilisi, Georgia, unpublished, 2012

[44] Mauldin, William, "Putin Pitches Russia to CEOs," October 18, 2011, Wall Street Journal, Putin is quoted as saying to a group of Global CEOs "All planned projects for modernizing the economy, for raising the effectiveness of government institutes: This is one of the priorities of our works – all these tasks will be carried out one after another, without question." No observers counter this opinion that Russia knows it must modernize, but how quickly and to what extent is the unknown.

[45] Mauldin, William, "Putin Pitches Russia to CEOs," October 18, 2011, Wall Street Journal, Chart in the article, with Source being Russia's Federal Statistics Service, shows FDI peaking in 2007 at nearly $30 Billion and sinking to under $15 Billion in 2010. 2011 figures for the first half of the year showed a path of less than $15B annually as well.

[46] Baramidze, Giorgi, "Georgia's Successful Transformation," Deputy Prime Minister of Georgia, Briefing presented at the George C Marshall Center January 2012, showed that FDI peaked in 2007 at $2B and was still less than half recovered by 2011, with $984M. Clearly the economic crisis has impacted these and Russia's figures, but the unrest caused by the 2008 Georgian-Russian war is undoubtedly a major influence as well.

28

[47] http://cpi.transparency.org/cpi2011/results/#CountryResults, Transparency International ranks Russia 143rd out of 182 nations for corruption

[48] Blank, Stephen J, "Georgia: The War Russia Lost," Military Review, 2008 Nov/Dec, "...the situation in Georgia...contributes significantly to investors' fears about russia's future economic health."

[49] Fidler, Stephen, "Over Dinner, Putin Takes Issue with Western Powers," November 12, 2011, Wall Street Journal, Putin was quoted as saying: "We think we are being squeezed out of the European energy market." The article goes on to state that the context was the new European rules forbidding ownership of pipelines by gas suppliers. This would be counter to Gazprom's business model, which has been to acquire as many national gas delivery systems as possible. The most recent case was Belarus, and Ukraine is in the cross-hairs.

[50] Per Concordiam, "Fueling Hope in Europe," 23 February 2011, 1(4), pg 48-51. Article quotes a June 2010 report produced for the Center for European Policy Studies that states "with U.S. markets awash with natural gas and prices plummeting.....LNG tankers have been rerouted to more lucrative markets in Europe, upsetting the status quo, with Gazprom losing market share." Since that article, U.S. shale extraction continues to keep North American prices suppressed nearly 1.5 years later. Nations such as Poland may also possibly have extensive shale gas reserves. This all has potential to disrupt Russian profits.

[51] Blank, Stephen J, "Georgia: The War Russia Lost," Military Review, 2008 Nov/Dec, as only one example, this article states that "Russia also does not seem upset that it has now lost any possibility of joining the World Trade Organization....."

[52] Racz, Andras, "Russian WTO Accession and the Geneva Agreements. Implications for Russia and Georgia," Dec 2011, Transatlantic Academy. Author extensively covers multitudes of ways Russia could exploit the seams of the agreement, even indicating "One may not exclude the possibility that once WTO accession is finally completed, the actual implementation of the Geneva agreement will be hampered, or even made impossible by Russia."

[53] Yepifantsev, Andrei, "Russia in Transcaucasia: What's Gone Wrong?" 24 Sept 2011, Russia in Global Affairs, Author states that "Armenia's increasing isolation is very dangerous. First, it plunges Yerevan into economic stagnation, which sooner or later will make the military potentials of Armenia and Azerbaijan so disparate that Baku will be able to hope for a Blitzkrieg in Karabakh." This is feasible. Many observers agree that Russia would defend Armenia-proper if it were attacked....but no one can be sure if Russians would be willing to die for Nagorno-Karabakh.

[54] Manoli, Panagiota, "Black Sea Regionalism in Perspective," December 2011, Center for International and European Studies, page 4, author states "Some schemes (i.e.....GUAM) have become obsolete..." A recent visit to the website http://guam-organization.org/en shows several meetings, but little in the way of concrete, substantive developments.

[55] Nation, Craig R, "Russia, the United States, and the Caucasus," Feb 2007, Congressional Research Series, Author states "For Years the United States has encouraged the development of the so-called GUUAM.....organization as a counter to Russian domination of the ...(CIS)." Since this article, the new acronym is GUAM, since Uzbekistan has already left the organization.

[56] Weekly Georgian Journal, "Value of Georgian Wine Export UP 37.7% in 2011," 2-8 February 2012, Page 12, Source: Georgian government organization Geostat. Article stated exports were highest in 5 years, but sales still lag behind pre-embargo levels for wine.

[57] Jane's Sentinel Country Risk Assessment, Georgia, Executive Summary, article states "The crisis in relations with Russia is estimated to have knocked 2.5% off the GDP growth rate between 2006 and the August 2008 war. The article did not cover GDP after the war, but it is without argument that GDP suffered additionally. Therefore, there is much to gain for Georgia to acquire full access to Russian markets once again.

[58] Georgia National Tourism Agency official statistics, http://www.gnta.ge/?61/statistics/&lan=en, Chart entitled "Travelers from Top 10 Countries and Market Ratios," shows 62,271 visitors from Russia, 8% of total for 2010, 4th highest behind Turkey, Azerbaijan and Armenia. For reference, USA was 6th

[59] Sidar, Cenk and Winrow, Gareth, "Turkey & South Stream: Turco-Russian Rapprochement and the Future of the Southern Corridor," 2011, Sidar Global Advisors. States that 3 million Russians visit Turkey each year, and that was before the liberalized visa policy started by Turkey, which allows Russians in for 30 days, VISA-free.

[60] Sidar, Cenk and Winrow, Gareth, "Turkey & South Stream: Turco-Russian Rapprochement and the Future of the Southern Corridor," 2011, Sidar Global Advisors. Author states: "The Russian authorities are also interested in the possibility of constructing an oil refinery and gas liquefaction plant at Ceyhan...." Georgia could stand to gain greatly if this investment could be diverted to a Georgian port.

[61] Georgian Business Week, "Georgia Will Receive 1.486 Billion Cubic Meters of Gas in 2012," February 7th 2012, Article quotes a Marika Valishvili document, (she is the Deputy Energy Minister) that states 85% will come from Azerbaijan, 14.2% from Russia and 8% from domestic production.

[62] Gronholt-Pederson, Jacob, "Turkey Approves Russian Gas Plan," Dec 29, 2011, Wall Street Journal,

[63] http://en.rian.ru/mlitary_news/20120124/170928027.html

[64] Dinmore, G and Segreti, G, "Berlusconi Quits Frontline Politics," Financial Times, February 4, 2012, article states "An animated Mr Berlusconi...showing a bruise he said came from playing ice hockey with Vladimir Putin...."

[65] Trukhachev, Vadim, "Strangely enough, Obama Praises Russia's Sworn Enemy," February 1, 2012, Pravda.Ru, Author, anti-Georgian, admits "What could (Georgia) be a model for? Perhaps the fight against corruption. ....The extent of everyday corruption was indeed reduced. It became easier to register a company, and investment poured into the country." He later quotes Vladimir Zharikhin of a think tank "Saakashvili is an enemy of Russia.....but in many ways he can be called an effective leader, and there is even something to be learned from him."

[66] Laruelle, Marlene, "Russia's Strategies in Afghanistan and their Consequences for NATO," Nov 2011, NATO Research Paper No 69. Author states of Russia and Afghanistan: "Both sides have sought to discuss the years 1950-1979 with a constructive voice and to ignore the decade of war." Beyond the article's statements, several engagements have taken place in several forums between Hamid Karzai and either Medvedev or Putin since Karzai came to power in Afghanistan.

[67] Weekly Georgian Journal, "Medvedev About Russian Military Bases," 9-15 February 2012, Medvedev is quoted as saying "....we have the data that (the) U.S. administration and...some of our neighboring states, continue to supply different kinds of arms to Georgia. That is why we had to bolster the military bases located on the territory of Abkhazia and S Ossetia." Outside of the scope of the article, from a geo-strategic point of view, it also makes sense to have forces on both sides of the main Caucasus range for military flexibility, since the mountain range could be considered an obstacle to expeditious military action.

[68] Zhemukhov, Sufian, "The Sovereign Trend. Russia's Victory Could Turn Into Defeat if it Continues its Neo-Colonial Policy," 2011, Caucasus Security Insight, National Institute for Strategic Studies. Author states: "...Georgia did not lose anything, apart from its illusions. Abkhazia and South Ossetia were de facto no longer its territories and it was only internal political logic that prevented the country's leaders from acknowledging that."

[69] Trenin, D (2009) Russia's Sphere's of Interest, Not Influence. The Washington Quarterly, 32(4), pp. 3-22

Bibliography :

1. Alessi, Christopher, "How Russia Can Benefit from the WTO," Dec 15, 2011, Council on Foreign Relations Analysis Brief

2. Anderson, Richard, "Europe's Dependence on Russian Natural Gas," Sep 2008, George C Marshall Center Occasional Paper Series #19

3. Aron, Leon, "Putin is Already Dead," Feb 7, 2012, Foreign Policy

4. Aslund, Anders, "Putin Without Putinism," Feb 8, 2012, Foreign Policy

5. Asmus, Ronald, "A Little War that Shook the World," 2010

6. Atlantic Council, "Georgia in the West: A Policy Road Map to Georgia's Euro-Atlantic Future," 2011

7. Babayan, Nelli and Shapovalova, Natalia, "Armenia: The Eastern Partnership's Unrequited Suitor," September 2011, FRIDE Policy Brief No 94

8. Badalyan, Lusine, "Interlinked Energy Supply and Security Challenges in the South Caucasus," 12 Dec 2011, Caucasus Analytical Digest No 33 (Sell pipeline to Russia)

9. Baev, Pavel K, "Military Reform Against Heavy Odds. Russia After the Global Economic Crisis," May 2010, pp. 169-185, Editors A Aslund, S. Guriev and A. Kuchins

10. Blank, Stephen J, "Georgia: The War Russia Lost," Military Review, 2008 Nov/Dec, pp 39-46

11. Bogomolov, A and Lytvynenko, O, "A Ghost in the Mirror: Russian Soft Power in Ukraine," January 2012, Chatham House Briefing Paper

12. Carnegie Endowment, Euro-Atlantic Security Initiative, "Missile Defense: Toward a New Paradigm," Feb 2012

13. Castillejo, Clare, "Improving European Policy Towards Fragile States," Sep 2011, FRIDE Policy Brief No 95

14. Caucasus Analytical Digest #29, September 2011

15. Caucasus Analytical Digest #30, October 2011

16. Caucasus Analytical Digest #31, November 2011

17. Cebeci, Munevver, "Issues in EU and US Foreign Policy," 2011 pg. 229-292

18. Charap, Samuel and Welt, Cory, "A New Approach to the Russia-Georgia Conflict," Oct 2010

19. Chicky, Jon E, "The Russian-Georgian War: Political and Military Implications for U.S. Policy," Feb 2009, Central Asia-Caucasus Institute

20. CIA World Factbook

21. Clover, Charles, "Russia's Military: Modern Warfare the Moscow Way," Feb 1, 2012, The Financial Times, pg 7

22. Collins James F and Rojansky, "Why Russia Matters: Ten Reasons Why Washington Must Engage Moscow," Aug 18, 2010, Foreign Policy

23. Cordesman, Anthony H, "The United States and Iran: Competition Involving Turkey and the South Caucasus," Aug 2011 DRAFT, Center for Strategic and International Studies

24. Cornell, Svante, "US Engagement in the Caucasus: Changing Gears," Helsinki Monitor, 2005

25. Cornell, Svante and Starr, Frederick, Editors, "The Guns of August 2008: Russia's War in Georgia," 2009.

26. Corso, Molly, "Georgia and the Sochi Olympics Games" 5 Dec 2011, Caucasus Analytical Digest No 32

27. CSIS-IND Conference Minutes, "Developing U.S. Strategy in the South Caucasus and Caspian Basin," June 24, 2010

28. Cullison, A, "Russia Slams New U.S. Ambassador," Wall Street Journal, Jan 19, 2012

29. Devdariani, Nikoloz, "An Engagement Strategy Towards the Occupied Territories: An Insight into Achievements," Georgia Today Issue No 599, Feb 10-Feb 16 2012

30. De Waal, Thomas, "The Caucasus, An Introduction," 2010

31. De Waal, Thomas, "Inviting the Unpredictable," 2011, Caucasus Security Insight, International Institute for Strategic Studies

32. East View Press, "Countdown to War in Georgia: Russia's Foreign Policy and Media Coverage of the Conflict in South Ossetia and Abkhazia," 2008

33. Fidler, S and Macdonald, A, "Europeans Retreat on Defense Spending," Aug 24, 2011, Wall Street Journal

34. Goksel, Nigar, "Turkish Policy Towards the Caucasus: A Balance Sheet of the Balancing Act," Black Sea Discussion Paper Series 2011/1, Center for Economic and Foreign Policy Studies

35. Gold, R, Gilbert D, and Dezember, R, "Glut Hits Natural Gas Prices," Jan 12, 2012, Wall Street Journal

36. Goldstone, Jack A, "Rise of the TIMBIs," Dec 2, 2011, Foreign Policy

37. Government of Georgia Report on the Aggression by the Russian Federation Against Georgia," Aug 2009

38. Government of Georgia, "Georgia National Security Concept," Tbilisi, Georgia, unpublished, 2012

39. Gronholt-Pederson, Jacob, "Turkey Approves Russian Gas Plan," Dec 29, 2011, Wall Street Journal

40. Iberi, David, "Georgia's Caucasus Strategy Revisited: Emerging Power in the South, Part 1," Jan 10, 2011, Jamestown Foundation Blog

41. Jarosiewicz, A and Strachota, K, "Nagorno-Karabakh – Conflict Unfreezing," Oct 26, 2011, Center for Eastern Studies, OSW Commentary No 65

42. Jones, James L, EUCOM Cdr, 8 March 2006, Statement Before the House Armed Services Committee

43. Judah, Kobzova and Popescu, "Dealing with a Post-BRIC Russia," Nov 2011, European Council on Foreign Relations

44. Kamp, Karl-Heinz, "NATO's Chicago Summit: A Thorny Agenda," NATO Research Paper No 70, November 2011 (For the foreseeable future, a true NATO missile defense system is – despite all the declarations – amore an ambition than a realistic prospect.)

45. Karasar, Hasan A, "Turkey and Russia Growing Closer Despite Cool History," Jan 30, 2012, The German Marshall Fund of the United States

46. Kassenova, Nargis, "Kazakhstan and the South Caucasus Corridor in the Wake of the Georgia-Russia War," Jan 2009, EU-Central Asia Monitoring No. 3

47. Kelkitli, Fatma A, "Russian Foreign Policy in South Caucasus Under Putin," Perceptions, Winter 2008

48. Khelashvili, George, "Georgian Perceptions of the North Caucasus and of U.S.-Russia Relations," PONARS Eurasia Policy Memo No 148, May 2011

49. Klein, Magarate, "Russia and the Arab Spring," Feb 2012, SWP Comments 3, German Institute for International and Security Affairs

50. Kolyander, Alexander, "Fitch Cuts Russia Outlook," Jan 16, 2012, Wall Street Journal

51. Kornilov, A and Suleymanov A, "Ankara's Eurasian Diplomacy," 2010, International Affairs #3, pp. 112-119

52. Kremenyuk, Victor, "Resetting and Disjunction," Russia in Global Affairs, April-June 2010

53. Larrabee, Stephen F, "Turkey's Eurasian Agenda," Winter 2011, The Washington Quarterly

54. Laruelle, Marlene, "Russia's Strategies in Afghanistan and their Consequences for NATO," Nov 2011, NATO Research Paper No 69

55. Lukyanov, Fyodor, "The Russian-Georgian War as a Turning Point," 24 Nov 2011, Russia in Global Affairs

56. Mankoff, Jeffrey, "The Russian Presidential Elections," Dec 20, 2011, Center for Strategic & International Studies

57. Manoli, Panagiota, "Black Sea Regionalism in Perspective," December 2011, Center for International and European Studies

58. Markedonov, Sergei, "History as a Weapon. The Circassian Issue Standing Between Russia and Georgia," 24 Sept 2011, Russia in Global Affairs

59. McFaul, Michael, "Transitions from Post-Communism," Journal of Democracy, Vol 16, No 3, July 2005, pp. 5-19

60. Meister, Stefan, "A New Start for Russian-EU Security Policy?" Genshagener Papiere No 7 July 2011, Genshagen Foundation and Land Brandenburg

61. Morar, Filon, "The Myth of Frozen Conflicts," June 2010, per Concordiam, pp. 10-17

62. Musabekov, Rasim, "Where Fields of Attraction Overlap. Azerbaijan Between Turkey and Russia," 24 Sept 2011, Russia in Global Affairs

63. Nation, Craig R, "Russia, the United States, and the Caucasus," Feb 2007, Congressional Research Series

64. Nation, Craig R, "Results of the 'Reset' in US-Russian Relations," July 2010, IFRI, pp.5-24

65. Nichol, Jim "Armenia, Azerbaijan and Georgia: Political Developments and Implications for U.S. Interests," April 15, 2011

66. Pearce, Katy E, "Poverty in the South Caucasus," 21 Dec 2011, Caucasus Analytical Digest No 34

67. Racz, Andras, "Russian WTO Accession and the Geneva Agreements. Implications for Russia and Georgia," Dec 2011, Transatlantic Academy

68. Racz, Andras, "Good Cop or Bad Cop? Russian Foreign Policy in the New Putin Era," January 2012, Transatlantic Academy

69. Remnick, David, "The Civil Archipelago. How Far Can the Resistance to Vladimir Putin Go?" Dec 19, 2011, The New Yorker

70. Roberts, Sean, r, "Kazakhstan and the United States: Twenty Years of Ambiguous Partnership," Atlantic Council ISSUEBRIEF, 2011

71. Rubin, Eric, "The South Caucasus: 20 Years of Independence," Speech at Carnegie Endowment for International Peace Conference, Nov 28, 2011

72. Saari, Sinikukka, "The Persistence of Putin's Russia," November 2011, The Finnish Institute of International Affairs

73. Sagdegh-Zadeh, "Iran's Strategy in the South Caucasus," Winter 2008, Caucasian Review of International Affairs, 2(1)

74. Sagramoso, Domitilla, "Jihad in the North Caucasus: Is There a Way Out?", 2011, Caucasus Security Insight, International Institute for Strategic Studies

75. Schaefer, Brett D and Kim, Anthony B, "U.S. Foreign Aid Recipients Show Little Support for America When Voting at the United Nations," April 6, 2010, Heritage Foundation 'Backgrounder' No 2395

76. Schroder, Henning, "Russia's National Security Strategy to 2020," Jun 2009, Russian Analytical Digest No 62, pp 6-10

77. Shevtsova, L. "Imitation Russia," Nov/Dec 2006, American Interest, pp. 67-77

78. Sidar, Cenk and Winrow, Gareth, "Turkey & South Stream: Turco-Russian Rapprochement and the Future of the Southern Corridor," 2011, Sidar Global Advisors

79. Simao, Licinia and Freire, Maria R, "The EU's Neighborhood Policy and the South Caucasus: Unfolding New Patterns of Cooperation," Caucasian Review of International Affairs, Vol 2(4) – Autumn 2008

80. Skakleyina, T.A. and Bogaturov, A.D, "The Russian Realist School of International Relations," March 2004, Communist and Post-Communist Studies, 37(1), pp. 37-51

81. Kosachev, K, "Values for the Sake of Unification," April 9, 2010, Russia in Global Affairs

82. Skyner, Louis, "Revising Russia's Energy Strategy," October 2011, Chatham House Briefing Paper

83. Soldatov, Andrei and Borogan, Irina, "The New Nobility," 2011

84. Stewart, Susan, "A Weaker Russia. Serious Repercussions for EU-Russia Relations," Sept 2011, SWP Comments, German Institute for International and Security Affairs

85. Thornburgh, Nathan, "Olympic Dreams" Time Magazine, 28 November 2011

86. Torello, Alessandro, "Nabucco Pipeline's Fate Hinges on Azerbaijan," Aug 1, 2011, Wall Street Journal

87. Trenin, D, "Russia's Spheres of Interest, Not Influence," 2009, The Washington Quarterly, 32(4). Pp. 3-22

88. Trenin, D, "Russia's Policy in the Middle East," 2010, The Century Foundation

89. Trenin, D, "Protests in Russia," Dec 29, 2011, Carnegie Endowment for International Peace

90. United States Government, "United States-Georgia Charter on Strategic Partnership," 9 January 2009

91. Valieva, Elizaveta, "Making Mischief," 2011, Caucasus Security Insight, International Institute for Strategic Studies

92. Vershbow, Alexander, "Georgia: One Year After the August War," US Ambassador, Asst Secretary of Defense for International Security affairs. Testimony Aug 4, 2009 to Senate Foreign Relations Committee,

93. Wall Street Journal, "Labor Union Imperialism, The AFL-CIO Targets Georgia," Jan 24, 2012

94. Wall Street Journal, "Which Dreams are Pipe Dreams," Dec 21, 2011

95. Wall Street Journal, "Russia Pipe Deals May Reassure EU as Winter Approaches," November 29, 2011

96. Winrow, Gareth, "Turkey, Russia and the Caucasus: Common and Diverging Interests," Nov 2009, Chatham House Briefing Paper

97. Yarlykapov, Akhmet, "Georgia Woos Its Neighbours," 2011, Caucasus Security Insight, International Institute for Strategic Studies

98. Yepifantsev, Andrei, "Russia in Transcaucasia: What's Gone Wrong?" 24 Sept 2011, Russia in Global Affairs

99. Zevelev, Igor, "Russia's Policy Toward Compatriots in the Former Soviet Union," 2008, Russia in Global Affairs, pp.49-62

100. Zikibayeva, Aigerim (Editor), "What Does the Arab Spring Mean for Russia, Central Asia, and the Caucasus?" Sept 2011, Center for Strategic and International Studies